How to Clown

Your Comprehensive Guide to Mastering the Art of Clowning

Henry Jestworth

Copyright © 2024 by Henry Jestworth

All rights reserved. No part of this book may be reproduced or used in any manner without the written permission of the copyright owner except for the use of quotations in a book review.

First paperback edition January 2024

ISBN: 9798877727694

www.invisibleropes.com

Table of Contents

Introduction 5
Chapter 1: Understanding Clowning 7
Chapter 2: Developing Your Clown Persona 11
Chapter 3: Mastering Basic Clown Skills 15
Chapter 4: The Art of Clown Makeup 21
Chapter 5: Crafting Your Clown Routine 25
Chapter 6: Crafting Your Clown Costume 29
Chapter 7: Interacting with Your Audience 33
Chapter 8: The Business of Clowning 37
Chapter 9: Safety and Ethics 41
Chapter 10: Overcoming Fears and Misconceptions 47
Chapter 11: Growing as a Clown 51
Chapter 12: Learning from the Greats 55
Chapter 13: Further Resources 59
Conclusion 61

Introduction

Welcome, dear reader, to the enchanting and whimsical world of clowning, a realm where laughter is the currency and joy knows no bounds. The art of clowning is an age-old tradition, a celebration of humor, theatrics, and the unabashed embrace of the fantastical. From the jesters who brought mirth to medieval courts to the iconic circus performers who graced the big tops with their colorful antics, clowning has endured as a universal language of delight that transcends cultural and linguistic barriers.

The Tradition of Clowning:

At its heart, clowning is a celebration of the human spirit's irrepressible desire to laugh and be entertained. It's a tradition that has woven itself into the fabric of history, offering respite during times of hardship and acting as a mirror to reflect the absurdities of the world. Think back to the classic antics of Charlie Chaplin's Tramp or the mischievous escapades of the Harlequin – these iconic characters have left an indelible mark on the art of clowning, reminding us that, regardless of the era, the pursuit of laughter is timeless.

Why Become a Clown?

As you embark on this journey into the heart of clowning, it's crucial to reflect on why you are drawn to this unique and captivating world. The reasons are as diverse as the spectrum of colors in a clown's costume. For some, it's the joy of spreading infectious laughter, creating moments of shared merriment that linger in the memories of both performer and audience. For others, the allure lies in the freedom to step outside the bounds of convention, embracing a world where silliness reigns supreme and creativity knows no limits.

Consider the story of Joseph Grimaldi, often hailed as the "father of modern clowning." In the early 19th century, Grimaldi captivated audiences with his physical comedy, eccentric costumes, and innovative use of makeup. His legacy not only shaped the trajectory of clowning but also left an enduring impact on the very essence of what it means to be a clown.

Navigating the Chapters:

As you leaf through the pages of this guide, imagine yourself stepping into oversized shoes, adorned in vibrant hues, and armed with a nose that promises a honk-worthy symphony. Our journey will be one of self-discovery and skill development, exploring the multifaceted facets of clowning, from understanding the nuances of different clown archetypes to crafting your unique clown persona.

Each chapter is a portal into a specific realm of the clowning universe. Whether you're intrigued by the art of applying clown makeup – transforming your face into a canvas of expression – or eager to master the delicate balance of entertaining various age groups, this guide will serve as your trusted companion.

So, buckle up your polka-dotted suspenders, adjust your oversized bowtie, and let the adventure unfold. The world of clowning awaits, and with each turn of the page, you'll find yourself inching closer to the magical intersection where laughter and artistry converge. Welcome to the grand spectacle of becoming a clown!

Chapter 1: Understanding Clowning

In the kaleidoscope of entertainment, where laughter reigns supreme and whimsy knows no bounds, the art of clowning stands as a timeless beacon of joy and merriment. As we embark on our journey to unravel the secrets of this captivating world, let us first delve into the heart of clowning, exploring its essence, various types, and the indispensable role it plays in weaving the tapestry of humor and entertainment.

Defining the Clown:

What is a clown? Is it the red-nosed, floppy-shoed figure with a penchant for slapstick, or is it a more nuanced character, capable of evoking a spectrum of emotions? Clowns, in their diverse forms, are performers who use physical comedy, exaggerated expressions, and a touch of absurdity to tickle the funny bone. From the auguste clown with its colorful and chaotic appearance to the classic whiteface clown, each type brings a unique flavor to the circus of laughter.

Consider Auguste, the mischievous troublemaker of the clown family. With oversized shoes and a knack for mischief, the Auguste is a master of physical comedy, embodying the chaotic energy that keeps audiences on the edge of their seats. On the flip side, the Whiteface, with its pristine and elegant makeup, exudes a refined sense of humor, relying on subtlety and precision to elicit laughter.

As you embark on your journey to become a clown, understanding the different types is not merely an academic exercise – it's a crucial step in shaping your unique identity under the big top. Picture yourself in the vibrant shoes of an Auguste, relishing in the chaos of playful antics, or imagine the elegance and precision required to embody the classic Whiteface. Knowing the distinctions helps you carve your niche, ensuring that your clown persona aligns with your personality and performance style.

Consider the practicalities of your chosen clown type: the costuming, makeup, and props. An Auguste might opt for mismatched, colorful attire that screams mischief, while a Whiteface might prefer a pristine, tailored ensemble. Your choice of costume and makeup is a tangible expression of your clown character, laying the groundwork for the delightful spectacle you'll bring to life.

The Role of Humor and Entertainment:

At its core, clowning is a celebration of laughter – the universal language that transcends barriers and binds people together in moments of shared delight. Humor, in the world of clowning, is a multifaceted gem, sparkling with satire, absurdity, and the unexpected. The great clowns of history understood this delicate dance between wit and whimsy.

Consider the timeless charm of Red Skelton, whose ability to blend physical comedy with heartfelt storytelling captivated audiences for decades. Through characters like Freddie the Freeloader, Skelton not only tickled funny bones but also touched hearts, showcasing how humor, when wielded with finesse, becomes a potent tool for both entertainment and connection.

Entertainment, in the realm of clowning, is an art form that transcends mere amusement. It's a symphony of laughter, surprise, and theatricality. Take, for instance, the legendary Charlie Chaplin. With his iconic Tramp character, Chaplin transformed silent comedy into a poignant narrative, highlighting the power of storytelling within the comedic domain. His performances were not just about making people laugh; they were about stirring emotions and leaving an indelible mark on the hearts of audiences worldwide.

For aspiring clowns, humor is your toolkit, and entertainment is your canvas. Practicality comes into play when you start crafting routines that resonate with your audience. Explore the physical comedy inherent in everyday actions – tripping over your own feet, struggling with an oversized prop – and infuse them with your unique comedic twist. The practical side of humor is about finding what makes you laugh and translating that into a language your audience can understand.

Consider practical exercises to hone your comedic timing and delivery. Work on your facial expressions in front of a mirror, experiment with different voices, and test out your physical gags. Remember, the best jokes often come from the authentic quirks and idiosyncrasies that make you, well, you.

Importance of Connecting with the Audience:

A clown's true magic lies in the ability to forge a genuine connection with the audience. It's more than just laughter; it's about creating moments that linger in the memories of those who witness the spectacle. A clown, in all their whimsical glory, is a conduit for shared experiences, a bridge between the ordinary and the extraordinary.

Consider the legendary Bozo the Clown, whose engaging presence and interactive style endeared him to generations of children. Bozo wasn't just a performer; he was a friend, an animated companion who made each child feel like the star of the show. The bond he forged with his audience went beyond the confines of the circus tent, illustrating the profound impact a clown can have on the hearts of those they entertain.

For a budding clown, the connection with your audience is not a theoretical concept; it's the heartbeat of your performance. Practicality here involves developing an awareness of your audience's reactions, adjusting your approach based on their energy, and inviting them into the interactive realm of clowning.

Consider practical strategies to engage your audience: make eye contact, use gestures that invite participation, and pay attention to the collective pulse of the room. A well-timed interaction, be it a playful wink or a shared chuckle, can transform your act from a performance to a shared experience.

So, as we step into the vast and colorful world of clowning, let us carry with us the understanding that clowns are not just jesters in makeup; they are architects of joy, weaving laughter into the very fabric of our lives. In the chapters to come, we'll explore the nuances of different clown types, the art of crafting a unique persona, and the skills that transform a clown from a mere entertainer to a cherished memory-maker. Get ready for a rollercoaster of hilarity and heart as we navigate the fascinating landscape of becoming a clown!

Chapter 2: Developing Your Clown Persona

In the vast world of clowning, your persona is the prism through which your unique light shines. This chapter is your compass as you embark on the exhilarating journey of crafting your clown identity – from choosing a name that resonates with whimsy to donning a distinctive costume and defining the very essence of your clown character.

Choosing a Clown Name:

Your clown name is more than just a label; it's a proclamation of your alter ego, the moniker that echoes in the hearts and minds of your audience. The right name sets the stage for the fantastical world you're about to create. Practicality meets creativity here – think about names that are easy to remember, pronounce, and, most importantly, reflect your character.

Consider the iconic Coco the Clown, whose name exudes playfulness and classic charm. Coco, with his timeless appeal, demonstrates how a well-chosen name becomes a calling card, leaving an indelible mark on the memories of those who witness the performance.

Some practical tips:

Test the Pronunciation: When selecting your clown name, choose one that's easy to pronounce. You want your audience to effortlessly roll your name off their tongues, adding to the accessibility and memorability of your persona.

Consider the Alliteration: Names with alliteration tend to be catchy and memorable. Think of Bubbles the Clown or Chuckles the Jester. Experiment with consonant sounds to create a name that bounces off the tongue.

Reflect Your Personality: Your clown name should reflect the essence of your character. If you're a whimsical, lighthearted performer, a name like Giggles might suit you. If you lean towards a more mysterious persona, consider something like MysticMime.

Creating a Unique Appearance:

Your appearance is the canvas upon which your clown persona is painted. It's not just about the costume and makeup; it's about creating a visual symphony that captivates the eyes and tells a story. As a budding clown, practicality comes into play when you consider the comfort and mobility of your costume, the durability of your makeup, and the functionality of your accessories.

Consider the timeless charm of Patch Adams, whose scrappy and mismatched attire complements his endearing personality.

Some practical tips:

Prioritize Comfort: Your costume should not only be a visual spectacle but also practical for movement. Opt for breathable fabrics, adjustable closures, and sturdy construction to ensure comfort throughout your performance.

Color Coordination Matters: Choose a color scheme that complements your character. Bright, contrasting colors often work well to capture attention. Consider the psychological impact of colors – red for energy, blue for calmness, and yellow for joy.

Functional Accessories: If your character incorporates accessories, ensure they are not just for show. Perhaps your oversized shoes could house a hidden pocket for small surprises, or your hat could double as a prop. Practical accessories add an extra layer of engagement to your act.

Defining Your Clown Character and Personality:

Your clown character is the beating heart of your performance. It's not just about the gags and routines; it's about breathing life into a persona that resonates with authenticity and charm. Practicality here involves introspection – who is your clown alter ego, and how does their personality manifest in the world of make-believe?

Consider the mischievous spirit of Krusty the Clown from The Simpsons, whose loveable flaws and quirks endear him to audiences young and old. List the characteristics of your clown persona – are they mischievous, shy, or exuberantly outgoing? What makes them tick, and how do they react to the absurdity of the clowning world? Your character's personality becomes the gravitational force that keeps your performance grounded and relatable.

Here are some other questions that will help you find your unique clown persona:

Create a Backstory: Give your clown a backstory. What's their origin? What motivates them? A well-defined character history helps you stay consistent in your portrayal and provides depth to your performance.

Identify Signature Moves: Every great clown has signature moves. Whether it's a distinctive dance, a catchphrase, or a unique way of interacting with the audience, having these trademark elements adds memorability to your act.

Connect with Your Authentic Self: Infuse elements of your own personality into your clown character. This connection not only makes your performance more authentic but also allows you to draw on personal experiences for relatable humor.

Other Practical Tips:

The following tips are always true, but incorporating them early on from the beginning of your journey will help you tremendously!

Practice Facial Expressions: Your face is your most powerful tool. Practice a range of facial expressions in front of a mirror to convey different emotions. A well-timed eyebrow raises or a quirky smile can enhance your comedic impact.

Experiment with Voice Modulation: Work on varying your voice pitch and tone. A versatile voice allows you to create different characters within your clown persona, adding depth to your performances.

Seek Feedback: Perform for friends or family and solicit constructive feedback. This outside perspective can help you refine your character and identify areas for improvement.

Record Your Performances: Recording your acts allows you to review and analyze your performance objectively. Pay attention to audience reactions, timing, and areas where you can inject more energy or humor.

As you embark on the exciting journey of developing your clown persona, remember that practicality and creativity dance hand in hand. Your clown name, appearance, and character are the threads that weave the tapestry of your clown identity. So, don your thinking cap, splash on some colorful imagination, and let the practical magic of crafting your clown persona begin!

Chapter 3: Mastering Basic Clown Skills

Welcome to the exciting world of honks, flops, and fantastical feats! In this chapter, we delve into the fundamental skills that define the quintessential clown. From the art of physical comedy to the dexterity of juggling, and the whimsy of balloon twisting to the colorful strokes of face painting, mastering these basic clown skills will not only bring joy to your audience but also elevate your performance to new heights.

As you embark on the exhilarating journey of mastering basic clown skills, envision yourself stepping into the ring, armed with oversized shoes, a vibrant costume, and a twinkle in your eye. These skills are the building blocks, the alchemy that turns ordinary moments into extraordinary laughter-filled memories.

Every clown worthy of the spotlight possesses a toolkit of essential skills that serve as the backbone of their comedic repertoire. Picture these skills as the colors on a clown's palette, waiting to be mixed and applied with finesse. In this chapter, we unravel the enchanting world of physical comedy and slapstick, the mesmerizing art of juggling, the whimsy of balloon twisting, and the canvas of face painting. Each skill is a portal into a realm where laughter reigns supreme.

Consider this chapter your compass, pointing you toward the fundamental skills that have been the bedrock of clowning for generations. However, this list is not a rigid prescription; it's an invitation to exploration. Take a deep breath and understand that each skill presented here is a gateway, a starting point for your own unique journey.

Also, embrace the learning process. To become a clown is to embrace the joy of learning. Picture yourself as a playful apprentice, discovering the nuances of each skill with wide-eyed curiosity. This chapter provides a roadmap, but the adventure is yours to mold. Dive into online tutorials, join local clubs, experiment with props, and paint smiles on imaginary faces. The skills you acquire will not only be tools in your clowning toolbox but also the threads that weave the tapestry of your unique performance.

So, dear reader, let the honks and giggles be your guide. Embrace the laughter that echoes in the footsteps of great clowns who came before you. As you navigate this chapter, remember that the joy is in the journey, the exploration, and the mastery that unfolds with each pratfall, juggle, twist, and stroke.

And now, let's review some skills.

Physical Comedy and Slapstick:

Mastering the Art of Falls: Practice controlled falls and trips. The key is to make it look accidental while ensuring your safety. Slapstick comedy thrives on exaggerated actions, so don't be afraid to go big with your reactions.

Facial Expressions and Gestures: Your face is a canvas for expression. Work on creating a range of facial expressions that amplify your comedic intentions. Combine these expressions with exaggerated gestures to enhance the humor.

Props for Laughs: Utilize everyday objects as props. A banana peel, a rubber chicken, or an oversized pair of glasses can turn mundane items into sources of amusement. The unexpected use of props adds an element of surprise to your physical comedy.

How to Learn:

Study Classic Comedians: Watch performances of iconic comedians like Charlie Chaplin, Buster Keaton, and Lucille Ball. Observe their timing, expressions, and use of physical comedy.

Improvise and Experiment: Find a safe space to experiment with physical comedy. Improvise scenarios, explore different movements and discover what elicits the most laughter.

Mirror Exercises: Stand in front of a mirror and practice your facial expressions and gestures. This helps you visualize how your actions appear to an audience.

Slow-Motion Rehearsals: Perform your routine in slow motion to analyze each movement. This allows you to identify areas for improvement and refine your comedic timing.

Example - The Imaginary Wall: Pretend to walk into an invisible wall. Use exaggerated movements and expressions to convey the impact. This classic routine never fails to bring laughter.

Juggling Basics:

Start with One Object: If you're new to juggling, begin with one item, like a beanbag or a scarf. Focus on developing a smooth and controlled throwing motion. Once you're comfortable with one, gradually add more items.

Practice in Front of a Mirror: Juggling requires hand-eye coordination. Practicing in front of a mirror allows you to observe and refine your technique. Pay attention to the height and rhythm of your throws.

Progress to More Complex Patterns: As you become proficient with basic juggling, challenge yourself with more complex patterns. Experiment with different types of juggling props, such as balls, clubs, or rings, to diversify your skill set.

How to Learn:

Online Tutorials: Explore online juggling tutorials on platforms like YouTube. Many tutorials break down juggling into step-by-step instructions, making it accessible for beginners.

Juggling Clubs or Classes: Join local juggling clubs or take classes. Learning alongside others provides motivation, and experienced jugglers can offer valuable tips.

Balloon Twisting:

Start with Simple Shapes: Begin with easy balloon shapes, like dogs, swords, or flowers. Focus on proper inflation and tying techniques. Mastering the basics sets the foundation for more intricate designs.

Learn Balloon Animal Anatomy: Understand the different segments of balloon animals – necks, bodies, and appendages. This knowledge is crucial for creating a variety of shapes and figures.

Balloon Twisting Flow: Practice transitioning smoothly from one twist to another. Balloon twisting is not just about individual shapes; it's about seamlessly combining twists to create dynamic and entertaining sculptures.

How to Learn:

Balloon Twisting Books: Invest in instructional books that provide step-by-step guides for various balloon sculptures. Books often include illustrations to help with visualizing each twist.

Online Courses: Enroll in online courses or watch tutorials that cover balloon twisting basics. Video demonstrations can be particularly helpful.

Basic Shapes Practice: Master basic shapes like dogs, swords, and flowers before moving on to more complex designs.

Time Trials: Challenge yourself to create specific shapes within a set time. This enhances speed and precision.

Face Painting:

Invest in Quality Face Paints: Opt for hypoallergenic, professional-grade face paints. They are safe for the skin and provide vibrant, long-lasting colors. Test the paints on a small area beforehand to ensure there are no adverse reactions.

Practice Basic Designs: Begin with simple face painting designs, such as butterflies, stars, or flowers. Focus on achieving clean lines and even coverage. As you gain confidence, you can gradually move on to more intricate patterns.

Personalize Your Designs: Tailor your face painting designs to suit your clown persona. Incorporate elements of your character, such as adding whimsical patterns or colors that match your costume. This personal touch enhances the overall thematic coherence of your performance.

How to Learn:

Face Painting Workshops: Attend face painting workshops or classes offered by experienced artists. Hands-on instruction allows for immediate feedback.

Online Resources: Explore online tutorials and resources that cover face painting techniques. Many artists share tips and tricks through video demonstrations.

Line and Detail Practice: Work on creating clean lines and intricate details. Practice painting straight lines, curves, and intricate patterns on a practice surface.

Remember, mastering these basic clown skills takes time and practice. Embrace the learning process with a playful spirit, and soon you'll be delighting audiences with your comedic prowess and artistic flair. The magic of clowning awaits, and these skills are your ticket to creating a performance that is as entertaining as it is unforgettable!

Chapter 4: The Art of Clown Makeup

Welcome to the transformative realm where the face becomes a canvas, and every stroke of color narrates a whimsical tale – the art of clown makeup. In this chapter, we embark on a journey that transcends the ordinary, exploring the nuances of choosing the right makeup, mastering the step-by-step application process, and learning the tricks to ensure your makeup remains as vibrant and captivating as your performance.

Clowns, with their undeniable range, have evolved from symbols of comic relief to beacons of mischief and even the bone-chilling antagonists of horror films. Their versatility makes them a popular choice for Halloween costumes. If you're not keen on a full Bozo the Clown ensemble, fear not. A clown makeup look can be a perfect alternative, and creating one is surprisingly easy. In collaboration with a talented makeup artist, we've crafted a three-step tutorial to guide you through the process.

But first -

Choosing the Right Makeup:

Selecting the perfect makeup is akin to choosing the colors for a masterpiece. The right palette not only enhances your features but also communicates the essence of your clown persona. Consider the following:

Quality Matters: Invest in professional-grade, hypoallergenic makeup. Quality products ensure skin safety and vibrant, long-lasting colors.

Bold and Bright: Clowns are known for their bold, expressive colors. Choose vibrant hues that align with your character. Reds, blues, yellows, and whites are classic choices that never fail to captivate.

Water-Based vs. Cream-Based: Water-based makeup is easy to apply and remove, making it suitable for beginners. Cream-based makeup provides a thicker, more opaque finish, ideal for creating intricate designs.

Applying Clown Makeup Step-by-Step:

The application of clown makeup is an art form that transforms the mundane into the extraordinary. Follow these step-by-step guidelines for a captivating result.

The first crucial step is to decide what kind of clown persona you wish to embody. Will you embrace the scariness of Twisty, the humor of Krusty, or perhaps the unsettling charm of a creepy clown? The choice is yours, and our makeup artist consultant poses a pivotal question: Are you fully committed to a character, or are you aiming for a 'cute' look?

As you contemplate your clown identity, prepare your face by applying a hydrating moisturizer and a layer of facial primer. The right primer ensures smooth application of the clown's signature all-over white base without any patchiness.

Step 1: Apply White Face Paint onto Your Entire Face

Using a dense and flat foundation brush, cover your entire face with white face paint. Applying a generous amount of product allows for a forgiving canvas, minimizing the risk of mistakes. It is recommended to use the back of the hand to warm up the white paint before carefully applying it to the forehead, eyelids, cheeks, chin, and hairline. Set the white face paint with a translucent setting powder.

Step 2: Draw Black Triangular Accents Above Your Eyebrows and Below the Bottom Lash Line

With thin paint brushes and black face paint, create tapering triangles above your eyebrows and below your lash line. We suggest emphasizing the importance of setting any cream product with a powder.

Step 3: Create Your Lip Look with Red Lipstick and Black Paint

Begin the lip look with an outline, starting at the center of the bottom lip and gliding upward along the bottoms of the apples of your cheeks. Fill in your lips with bright red lipstick for longevity. If you want to intensify your clown look, sweep the red lipstick onto your cheeks and buff it out using a medium-sized, angled contour brush. This optional step adds an extra touch of whimsy to your clown ensemble.

If you prefer a simpler plan, here are the basic must-haves of clown makeup, split into 5 simple steps:

Start with a Clean Canvas: Begin with a clean, moisturized face. This ensures an even application and prevents makeup from settling into fine lines.

Apply a White Base: Use a sponge or brush to apply a white base. This serves as the foundation for your design, making other colors pop.

Define Features with Color: Choose vibrant colors to define the eyes, nose, and mouth. Reds for the nose, blues for the eyes, and a bold outline for the mouth create a classic clown look.

Add Details and Accents: Let your creativity flow as you add details such as dots, swirls, or highlights. These accents contribute to the uniqueness of your clown persona.

Set with Powder: Gently apply a translucent setting powder to set the makeup. This reduces shine and helps the colors stay vibrant throughout your performance.

Tips for Maintaining Makeup During Performances:

Maintaining your makeup's allure during the energetic whirlwind of performance requires a blend of preparation and quick fixes. Consider these tips:

Invest in Setting Spray: A setting spray helps your makeup withstand sweat and movement. Lightly mist your face before hitting the stage for added durability.

Carry Touch-Up Essentials: Pack a small kit with essentials like a makeup sponge, extra colors, and powder for on-the-go touch-ups. Be prepared for quick fixes between acts.

Avoid Touching Your Face: Minimize touching your face to prevent smudging. If you need to wipe away sweat, use a gentle patting motion with a clean tissue.

Practice Removal Techniques: Efficient makeup removal is as crucial as its application. Experiment with different removal methods to find what works best for your skin type.

Know Your Makeup's Limits: Understand the limitations of your makeup in different conditions. If you anticipate intense physical activity, consider opting for a more durable, long-wearing product.

As you delve into the art of clown makeup, remember that your face is your most powerful prop. Let the colors tell the story of your character, and with each stroke, unveil the enchanting world that lies behind the mask. The canvas is yours, dear clown, so paint it with laughter and make every expression a masterpiece!

Chapter 5: Crafting Your Clown Routine

The clown's artistry extends beyond makeup and costume; it's in the choreography of laughter, the dance of gags, and the rhythm of whimsy. In this chapter, we delve into the intricacies of crafting a clown routine that leaves a lasting impression. From the grandeur of your entrance to the carefully structured acts, the spontaneous burst of improvisation, and the selection of props and gags, every element contributes to the symphony of joy that is a well-crafted clown performance.

Creating a Memorable Entrance:

The entrance sets the stage for the enchantment to come. Consider these elements to ensure your grand arrival is a spectacle in itself:

Music and Sound: Choose a lively and fitting soundtrack that complements your character. The right music builds anticipation and sets the tone for your performance.

Physicality: Embrace exaggerated movements and gestures. Your entrance is not just a walk; it's a performance in itself. Consider a skip, a hop, or a comically slow saunter to captivate your audience from the moment you step into the spotlight.

Surprises and Props: Consider incorporating surprise elements or props into your entrance. A confetti cannon, a small explosion of streamers, or an oversized prop can add an element of surprise and set a jubilant tone.

Structuring a Clown Act:

A well-structured clown act is a journey, taking your audience through peaks of laughter and valleys of delightful suspense. Consider the following components:

Opening Gag: Start with a strong opening gag to grab attention and establish your character. This could be a visual joke, a surprising gesture, or even a well-timed pratfall.

Comic Routines: Plan comedic routines that showcase your unique clown persona. Whether it's a quirky dance, a series of amusing interactions with imaginary friends, or a hilarious attempt at a simple task, let your creativity shine.

Interactive Moments: Involve the audience in your act. Whether through playful banter, inviting volunteers, or responding to audience reactions, creating interactive moments fosters a sense of shared joy.

Climactic Finish: Build toward a climactic finish that leaves a lasting impression. This could be a visually stunning trick, a surprising transformation, or a final burst of laughter-inducing chaos.

Incorporating Improvisation:

Clowning is an art form that thrives on spontaneity and connection with the audience. Here's how to incorporate improvisation into your routine:

Read the Audience: Pay attention to audience reactions and energy. Adapt your performance based on their responses, and be ready to seize unexpected moments for impromptu gags.

Interactive Improv: Engage in interactive improv with the audience. Respond to their cues, play off their reactions, and weave their contributions into the fabric of your routine.

Adaptability: Embrace the unexpected. If a prop malfunctions or a planned gag takes an unexpected turn, use it to your advantage. The beauty of clowning lies in the ability to turn mishaps into moments of hilarity.

Selecting Appropriate Props and Gags:

The right props and gags are the tools of your trade, enhancing the comedic magic of your performance. Consider the following when selecting and utilizing them:

Match with Your Character: Choose props that align with your clown persona. Whether it's a comically oversized umbrella, a squirting flower, or a miniature bicycle, each prop should enhance the narrative of your character.

Versatility: Opt for props that offer versatility. A simple prop can be used in various ways, creating different comedic moments throughout your routine.

Timing is Key: Master the art of comedic timing with your props and gags. Whether it's the unexpected reveal of a hidden prop or the precise moment for a visual gag, timing enhances the comedic impact.

Finding Inspiration for a Clown Routine:

Now we know what you are thinking: easier said than done, right? Well, we never said that crafting your own unique routine would be easy!

Here are some ways you can start:

Watch and Learn: Dive into the world of clowning by watching performances of renowned clowns from different eras. Study their styles, comedic timing, and the way they connect with the audience. Classic clowns like Charlie Chaplin, and Emmett Kelly, and contemporary performers offer a treasure trove of inspiration.

Attend Live Performances: Experience live clown performances whenever possible. Attend circuses, street performances, or local theater shows that feature clowns. Observing the live interaction between clowns and the audience can spark creative ideas.

Explore Different Genres: Clowns come in various styles, from classic circus clowns to theatrical or even avant-garde performers. Explore different genres of clowning to find what resonates with you. Whether it's silent physical comedy, slapstick, or a more theatrical approach, each style offers unique possibilities.

Tap into Personal Experiences: Your own life experiences can be a rich source of inspiration. Think about funny or memorable moments from your past, childhood games, or even everyday situations that can be exaggerated and transformed into comedic routines.

Collaborate and Brainstorm: Brainstorm ideas with fellow performers, friends, or even a mentor if possible. Collaborative sessions can spark creativity, and diverse perspectives may offer new angles for your routine.

As you craft your clown routine, remember that every act is a unique expression of your creativity and connection with the audience. Let the laughter flow organically, embrace the unexpected, and paint the stage with the vibrant strokes of your clowning prowess. The world is your circus, and with each routine, you become the ringmaster of joy under the big top!

Chapter 6: Crafting Your Clown Costume

The clown costume is a vivid canvas that paints the first strokes of humor and sets the tone for an unforgettable performance. Whether you're a seasoned performer or a newcomer to the world of clowning, crafting the perfect costume is an art form that goes beyond the mere donning of oversized shoes and a colorful wig. Let's delve into the essential features, tips, and recommendations that will guide you in creating a captivating clown ensemble and enhance your comedic presence under the spotlight.

Essential Features of a Clown Costume:

Oversized Clothing: Clown costumes often feature exaggerated, oversized clothing to create a whimsical and humorous appearance. Consider baggy pants, a roomy shirt, and an oversized jacket to achieve the classic clown silhouette.

Bright and Bold Colors: Vibrant colors are the hallmark of a clown costume. Choose a color palette that reflects your character – whether it's the classic red, yellow, and blue or a more avant-garde combination. The goal is to be visually striking and attention-grabbing.

Unique Patterns and Prints: Incorporate unique patterns and prints to add visual interest to your costume. Polka dots, stripes, or checkerboard patterns are popular choices that can enhance the playful nature of your character.

Mismatched Accessories: Clowns often wear mismatched accessories like gloves, socks, and shoes. This intentional disarray adds to the comedic effect and reinforces the carefree spirit of clowning.

Colorful Wig and Makeup: A brightly colored wig is a staple for many clowns. It adds flair to your appearance and complements your makeup. Speaking of which, clown makeup is an essential part of the costume, often featuring exaggerated features like a red nose, painted-on smile, and expressive eyes.

Big, Silly Shoes: Oversized, goofy shoes are iconic in clown costumes. Choose comfortable yet exaggerated footwear that suits your character. Some clowns even opt for shoes with squeakers to add an extra layer of comedy.

Tips and Recommendations:

Reflect Your Character: Your costume is an extension of your clown persona. Consider your character's personality, traits, and the type of performances you'll be doing when selecting colors, patterns, and accessories.

Comfort is Key: While the visual impact of your costume is crucial, don't overlook comfort. Clown performances can be physically demanding, so ensure that your costume allows for ease of movement and doesn't hinder your ability to perform.

Accessorize Creatively: Accessories are a fantastic way to inject personality into your costume. Think oversized bow ties, quirky hats, or even a colorful umbrella. Experiment with accessories that enhance your character's story and add a touch of individuality.

Consider Practicalities: Depending on the nature of your performances, consider practical aspects like the breathability of fabrics, ease of cleaning, and the durability of your costume. This becomes especially important for clowns who engage in physical comedy or outdoor performances.

DIY and Thrifting: Crafting your own costume can be a rewarding and cost-effective option. Visit thrift stores for unique finds, and don't hesitate to get creative with DIY elements. Your costume doesn't have to be brand new; it just needs to reflect your clowning spirit.

Additional Considerations:

Seek Inspiration: Look for inspiration from established clowns, both classic and contemporary. Study their costumes, makeup, and overall presentation to gain insights into the diverse possibilities within the world of clowning.

Experiment and Evolve: Your first costume may not be your last. As you evolve as a clown and refine your character, feel free to experiment with different elements of your costume. The beauty of clowning lies in its ability to adapt and evolve.

Connect with the Community: Joining clown communities and forums can provide valuable insights and feedback. Share your costume ideas, seek advice, and learn from the experiences of fellow clowns who have walked the path of crafting their own signature look.

Remember, your clown costume is not just an outfit; it's a visual representation of the joy and laughter you bring to your audience. So, embrace the creative process, have fun with your costume choices, and let your clown ensemble become a living, breathing expression of the delightful world you create under the big top.

Chapter 7: Interacting with Your Audience

The heart of clowning beats in the laughter of the audience, and the artistry lies not just in the performance but in the magical connection forged with those who share the spotlight under the big top. In this chapter, we delve into the delicate dance of interacting with your audience, exploring the nuances of reading their cues, gracefully handling hecklers and challenging situations, and mastering the art of engaging both children and adults in the joyous spectacle of clowning.

Reading Your Audience:

Step into the spotlight with a discerning eye and an open heart. Reading your audience is the delicate art of understanding their collective mood and responding with the infectious joy that defines clowning.

Observation Skills - Sharpen your observational skills to read the mood of your audience. Observe their body language, facial expressions, and overall energy. A responsive clown is a tuned-in clown.

Laughter as a Guide - Laughter is the compass of the clown. Pay attention to the intensity and timing of laughter. It signals what resonates with the audience and guides you in adjusting your performance.

Adaptability - Be adaptable to the dynamics of different audiences. What works with one group may not with another. Embrace the fluidity of your performance to suit the vibe of each crowd.

Interactive Moments - Create intentional interactive moments that invite audience participation. Whether it's a shared joke, a playful gesture, or a call-and-response routine, these moments enhance connection.

Handling Hecklers and Difficult Situations:

In the realm of live performance, hecklers may occasionally test your mettle, but a seasoned clown navigates these challenges with grace and humor. Approach hecklers not as adversaries, but as potential collaborators in the laughter you're weaving.

Stay Calm and Composed - Hecklers are part of live performances, but your response sets the tone. Stay calm and composed. Avoid escalating the situation and maintain professionalism.

Incorporate Humor - Diffuse tension with humor. Instead of confronting a heckler, incorporate their comment into your routine in a light-hearted manner. Turning it into a joke can win the audience over.

Redirect Attention - Redirect attention away from the heckler. Engage with other audience members, involve them in the routine, and shift the focus back to the positive energy of the performance.

Involve Security or Staff - If a situation escalates, involve security or venue staff. Your priority is the safety and enjoyment of the audience. Professional intervention ensures a smooth continuation of the show.

Engaging with Children and Adults:

The circus tent is a diverse tapestry of young laughter and seasoned smiles. Engaging both children and adults requires the finesse of adapting your performance to cater to different sensibilities. From eye-level connections with the little ones to sophisticated banter that resonates with adults, the art lies in finding the balance.

Adapt Your Performance - Tailor your performance to be inclusive of both children and adults. Include visual gags that appeal to younger audiences while incorporating subtle humor for adults.

Eye Contact and Proximity - Connect with children through eye contact and proximity. Get down to their eye level, and use facial expressions and gestures to make them feel part of the fun.

Interactive Games - Incorporate interactive games that involve children. Simple games, such as imaginary ball tossing or mimicking your movements, create a sense of participation and joy.

Respect Personal Space - Be mindful of personal space when interacting with both children and adults. Some may enjoy close interaction, while others prefer a bit of distance. Gauge comfort levels and adjust accordingly.

Encourage Adult Participation - Engage adults by incorporating sophisticated humor and witty banter. Adults often enjoy feeling included in the playful world of clowning, so encourage their participation in a way that respects their sensibilities.

Remember, the magic of clowning lies not just in the jokes and routines but in the shared experience with your audience. Whether young or old, every member of the audience contributes to the tapestry of joy that unfolds under the circus tent. Embrace the diversity of your audience, respond to their cues with grace, and let the laughter weave a connection that transcends the boundaries between the stage and the stands.

Chapter 8: The Business of Clowning

Embarking on the business side of clowning is the curtain call that brings your whimsical world into the realm of professionalism. In this chapter, we explore the practical aspects of setting up your clown business, crafting an effective marketing strategy to showcase your unique brand of joy, determining pricing structures, navigating the delicate art of negotiation, and considering crucial legal aspects that safeguard both you and your clients.

Setting Up a Clown Business:

Starting the whimsical journey of professional clowning involves more than just honking noses and oversized shoes—it's a business venture that demands thoughtful planning. In this section, we delve into the nuts and bolts of setting up your clown business, exploring key considerations from choosing the right business structure to maintaining a vibrant inventory of costumes and props. Whether you're a solo performer or envisioning a clowning empire, these foundational steps lay the groundwork for a successful and sustainable venture.

Business Structure - Choose a suitable business structure for your clowning venture, whether it's a sole proprietorship, partnership, LLC, or corporation. Each structure has different implications for taxes, liability, and operations. There is no one answer here - you should decide based on your specific situation, geographic location, and plans for the future. If there is any doubt, discuss this topic with a professional before deciding.

Business Plan - Develop a comprehensive business plan that outlines your goals, target market, services offered, and financial projections. A well-thought-out plan serves as a roadmap for your clowning venture.

Insurance - Explore insurance options to protect yourself and your clients. Liability insurance is particularly important for performers. Consult with insurance professionals to tailor coverage to your specific needs.

Costume and Prop Inventory - Establish an inventory of costumes, makeup, and props needed for your performances. Regularly update and maintain your inventory to ensure you're well-prepared for various events.

Marketing Yourself as a Clown:

As a clown, your ability to spread joy hinges on your visibility and appeal. This section unveils the secrets to marketing yourself effectively as a clown, transforming your unique brand of whimsy into a sought-after spectacle. From crafting a professional brand identity to building a captivating online presence and navigating the world of networking, these strategies will elevate your clown persona from a local delight to a household name.

Create a Professional Brand - Develop a professional brand that reflects your unique clown persona. A captivating logo, vibrant colors, and a cohesive visual identity contribute to a memorable brand image.
Online Presence:

Build a strong online presence through a website and social media platforms. Showcase your portfolio, highlight client testimonials, and use engaging content to connect with potential clients.

Networking - Network within the entertainment industry and local communities. Attend events, collaborate with other performers, and establish relationships with event planners, schools, and businesses.

Promotional Materials - Invest in high-quality promotional materials, including business cards, flyers, and promotional videos. These materials serve as valuable tools for marketing your clowning services.

Pricing and Negotiating Contracts:

Determining the right price for your laughter-filled performances is an art in itself. In this section, we explore the intricacies of pricing and negotiating contracts as a professional clown. With insights into researching market rates, creating transparent packages, and honing negotiation skills, you'll be equipped to strike the perfect balance between the value of your art and the expectations of your clients.

Research Market Rates - Research market rates for clowning services in your region. Consider factors such as the type of event, duration of performance, and your level of expertise when determining your pricing.

Create Transparent Packages - Develop transparent packages outlining what each service includes. Clearly communicate your pricing structure to clients, specifying any additional costs for travel, special requests, or extended performances.

Negotiation Skills - Hone your negotiation skills to find mutually beneficial agreements with clients. Be flexible while maintaining the value of your services. Consider bundling services or offering discounts for long-term contracts.

Legal Considerations:

Behind the scenes of every clown's vibrant performance lies a backdrop of legal considerations that safeguard both the artist and the audience. This section illuminates the legal aspects of clowning, from crafting solid contracts and protecting intellectual property to securing necessary permits and understanding tax obligations. Navigating these legal waters ensures a harmonious and legally sound journey under the big top.

Contracts - Draft clear and comprehensive contracts for your performances. Specify details such as date, time, location, services provided, and payment terms. Having a solid contract protects both parties and ensures a smooth business relationship.

Intellectual Property - Understand and protect your intellectual property rights. If you create unique characters, routines, or shows, consider trademarking or copyrighting your work to prevent unauthorized use.

Permits and Licenses - Check local regulations regarding permits and licenses for public performances. Ensure compliance with any necessary permits to avoid legal issues during events.

Tax Obligations - Familiarize yourself with tax obligations for self-employed individuals (or based on your selected way of operating). Keep thorough records of your income and expenses, and consult with a tax professional to ensure compliance with tax laws.

As you step into the business side of clowning, remember that professionalism and a well-organized approach enhance not only your success but also the overall perception of the clowning industry. Balancing the joy of performance with the practicalities of business ensures a sustainable and fulfilling journey under the big top.

Chapter 9: Safety and Ethics

Within the colorful tapestry of clowning, safety and ethics form the sturdy threads that weave the fabric of a responsible and respectful performance. This chapter delves into the paramount importance of ensuring safety during your whimsical acts, offering guidance on handling sensitive topics with care and exploring the imperative of respecting cultural and social boundaries. As a custodian of joy, it is your ethical duty to create an environment where laughter thrives without compromising the well-being, emotions, or beliefs of your audience.

Ensuring Safety During Performances:

Safety is the silent guardian behind every burst of laughter in the world of clowning. As you step into the spotlight, it's not just about the gags and pranks; it's about creating an environment where joy thrives without compromise. In this section, we unravel the crucial aspects of ensuring safety during your performances.

Performance Space Assessment - Conduct thorough assessments of performance spaces to identify potential hazards. From tripping hazards to secure rigging, ensuring a safe environment is paramount for both performers and the audience.

Costume and Prop Safety - Regularly inspect and maintain costumes and props to mitigate any risks of accidents. From secure fastenings to well-constructed props, prioritizing safety in the design and maintenance of your clowning essentials is non-negotiable.

Audience Interaction Guidelines - Establish clear guidelines for audience interaction to avoid unintentional discomfort or injury. Communicate boundaries, seek consent, and ensure that any participatory elements are designed with the safety of both the performer and the audience in mind.

Handling Sensitive Topics with Care:

Clowning is an art of universal joy, and with that comes the responsibility of navigating sensitive topics with utmost care and consideration. In this section, we delve into the nuanced world of handling sensitive topics with care, whether it involves cultural themes, gender considerations, or the intricacies of sensitive humor. Laughter should be a unifying force, and approaching these topics with sensitivity ensures that your performance fosters appreciation, understanding, and inclusivity.

Cultural Sensitivity - Approach cultural themes with sensitivity and respect. Be mindful of cultural nuances, stereotypes, and potential misinterpretations to ensure that your performance fosters appreciation rather than perpetuates stereotypes. Gender and Identity Considerations:

Navigate themes related to gender and identity with care. Avoid reinforcing stereotypes or making assumptions about individuals based on their appearance. Foster an inclusive environment that celebrates diversity.

Sensitive Humor - Exercise discretion when incorporating sensitive topics into your humor. Whether it's political, religious, or personal, gauge your audience and approach such topics with tact and consideration, ensuring that laughter remains a unifying force rather than a divisive one.

Respecting Cultural and Social Boundaries:

The spotlight of clowning extends far beyond individual performances; it reaches into the diverse landscapes of cultures and social contexts. This section explores the imperative of respecting cultural and social boundaries, emphasizing the importance of research, understanding, and inclusive language. Your clowning journey is a bridge between hearts, and by navigating the rich tapestry of cultural nuances, you transform your performances into a celebration that transcends language and resonates universally.

Research and Understanding - Prioritize research and understanding of the cultural and social contexts in which you perform. Tailor your acts to be respectful of local customs, traditions, and sensitivities, ensuring that your clowning transcends language and resonates universally.

Inclusive Language and Humor - Utilize inclusive language and humor that welcomes audiences from diverse backgrounds. Avoid language or actions that may be exclusionary, offensive, or alienating to certain groups.

Consent and Audience Comfort - Prioritize consent and the comfort of your audience. Be attuned to non-verbal cues and adjust your performance accordingly. Ensure that your clowning space is one where everyone feels welcome, valued, and included.

The Clown's Oath:

The Clowns of America organization has created The Eight Clown Commandments. It can be summed up in the following oath:

> *I do hereby promise that while in Clown makeup and costume, I will not swear, use abusive language, smoke, use drugs or drink alcoholic beverages. I will always look my best when in makeup and will always stay in a full wardrobe while in public. I will always bend to entertain a child or person less fortunate and will treat all with dignity and happiness.*

The full list of clown commandments:

1. I will keep my acts, performance, and behavior in good taste while I am in costume and makeup. I will remember at all times that I have been accepted as a member of the clown club only to provide others, principally children, with clean clown comedy entertainment. I will remember that a good clown entertains others by making fun of himself or herself and not at the expense or embarrassment of others.
2. I will learn to apply my makeup in a professional manner. I will provide my own costume. I will carry out my appearance and assignment for the entertainment of others and not for personal gain or personal publicity when performing for either the International club or alley events. I will always try to remain anonymous while in makeup and costume as a clown, though there may be circumstances when it is not reasonably possible to do so.
3. I will neither drink alcoholic beverages nor smoke while in makeup or clown costume. Also, I will not drink alcoholic beverages prior to any clown appearances. I will conduct myself as a gentleman/lady, never interfering with other acts, events, spectators, or individuals. I will not become involved in or tolerate sexual harassment or discrimination on the basis of race, color, religion, sex, national origin, age, disability, or any protected status.
4. I will remove my makeup and change into my street clothes as soon as possible following my appearance so that I cannot be associated with any incident that may be detrimental to the good name of clowning. I will conduct myself as a gentleman/lady at all times.
5. While on appearance in makeup and costume, I will carry out the directives of the producer or his designated deputies. I will abide by all performance rules without complaint in public.
6. I will do my very best to maintain the best clown standards of makeup, costuming, properties, and comedy.
7. I will appear in as many clown shows as I possibly can.

8. I will be committed to providing an atmosphere free of discrimination and harassment for clowns of all ages to share ideas and learn about the art of clowning.

Embracing the ethical dimensions of clowning elevates your artistry to a level where laughter is not just a sound but a shared experience that unites hearts. As you navigate the vast spectrum of emotions and themes within your performances, let safety and ethical considerations be the guiding stars that illuminate the path to joy under the big top.

Chapter 10: Overcoming Fears and Misconceptions

Beyond the laughter and whimsy, the world of clowning has faced its fair share of fears and misconceptions. In this chapter, we confront these apprehensions head-on, addressing common fears associated with clowns, challenging persistent stereotypes, and advocating for positive clowning experiences. It's time to unravel the layers of misunderstanding that have cast shadows on the vibrant art of clowning and illuminate the path toward a more nuanced and joyful perception.

Addressing Common Fears Associated with Clowns:

The fear of clowns, known as coulrophobia, has cast a shadow over the colorful world of clowning. Acknowledge and address coulrophobia with empathy and understanding. Delve into the roots of this fear, and explore strategies to create a clowning environment that feels safe and enjoyable for everyone.

Recognize that some individuals may have genuine fears or anxieties related to clowns. Implement accessibility considerations, such as providing advance information about clown performances, to ensure a positive experience for all audience members.

Challenging Stereotypes:

Beyond the makeup and costumes lies a rich tapestry of diverse clown personas and artistic expressions. Challenge stereotypes by showcasing the multifaceted nature of clowns. Explore and celebrate the diversity of clown personas, from classic circus clowns to theatrical and avant-garde performers. By embracing a range of clowning styles, we break down limiting stereotypes.

Highlight that clowns are more than makeup and costumes; they are skilled performers who bring joy through a variety of artistic expressions. Challenge the notion that clowns are solely associated with exaggerated features and showcase the depth and artistry within the clowning community.

Advocating for Positive Clowning Experiences:

To advocate for positive clowning experiences is to champion joy and inclusivity. By collaborating with local organizations, offering educational content, and showcasing the diverse representations of clowns, we aspire to reshape the narrative surrounding clowning and foster a greater appreciation for the transformative and positive impact it brings to audiences.

To become a 'brand' in your local area and promote the art form in general, try to engage with communities to foster positive perceptions of clowning. Collaborate with local organizations, schools, and events to showcase the uplifting and entertaining aspects of clown performances, fostering a sense of community joy.

If possible, launch educational initiatives to demystify clowning and provide insights into the art form. Offer workshops, presentations, or online content that explains the history, skills, and positive impact of clowns, dispelling myths and fostering a greater appreciation for the craft.

Advocate for inclusivity within the clowning community. Promote the idea that clowns can represent a wide spectrum of cultures, identities, and styles, creating a more inclusive and relatable image that resonates positively with diverse audiences.

By unraveling the fears and misconceptions surrounding clowns, we seek to redefine the narrative and illuminate the authentic joy that resides at the heart of the clowning world. It's time to encourage a broader understanding of the art form, ensuring that audiences can embrace the transformative and positive experiences that skilled clowns bring to the stage.

Chapter 11: Growing as a Clown

The journey of a clown is one of perpetual growth and evolution. In this final chapter, we explore avenues for continuous development, both professionally and personally. From embracing ongoing education and training to becoming an active member of clown communities and organizations, we unravel the threads that weave a vibrant tapestry of growth for any dedicated clown.

Just as a garden flourishes with careful cultivation, a clown's craft blossoms through continuous refinement. The pages to follow will illuminate the avenues for learning, from workshops and masterclasses to the enriching embrace of clown communities. These recommendations aim not only to enhance your skills but also to invigorate your passion and commitment, ensuring that each step in your clowning journey is a joyous leap toward perpetual improvement.

Continuing Education and Training:

The laughter that emanates from the clown's heart is a reflection of an ever-evolving journey of growth. Continuing education and training are essential pillars of a clown's developmental voyage.

Workshops and Masterclasses - Embrace opportunities for workshops and masterclasses to refine your skills and explore new dimensions of clowning. Seek out experienced mentors and trainers who can offer insights, techniques, and fresh perspectives to enhance your craft.

Skill Diversification - Continuously diversify your clowning skill set. Whether it's learning new juggling tricks, mastering different styles of physical comedy, or delving into new forms of clowning, the pursuit of varied skills adds depth and versatility to your performances.

Joining Clown Communities and Organizations:

Beyond the solitary spotlight, the world of clowning thrives in the shared glow of community. Joining clown communities and organizations is not only expanding professional networks but also fostering collaboration, inspiration, and a collective sense of support within the vibrant tapestry of the clowning world.

Networking Opportunities - Become an active member of clown communities and organizations to expand your network and connect with fellow performers. Attend gatherings, conferences, and online forums to share experiences, gain inspiration, and build a supportive network within the clowning community.

Collaborative Projects - Collaborate on projects with fellow clowns. Joining forces with other performers can lead to innovative ideas, shared resources, and a sense of camaraderie that enhances your growth as a clown and enriches the overall clowning landscape.

Balancing a Clowning Career with Personal Life:

The laughter a clown shares with the world is a gift, but maintaining a harmonious balance between the spotlight and the sanctuary of personal life is an art in itself.

Establishing Boundaries - Set clear boundaries between your clowning career and personal life. Define specific times for performances, rehearsals, and downtime to ensure that both aspects of your life thrive without encroaching on each other.

Self-Care Practices - Prioritize self-care practices to maintain a healthy balance. Clowning is demanding, both physically and emotionally, and taking care of your well-being ensures that you bring your best self to every performance and also enjoy a fulfilling personal life.

<u>Quality Over Quantity</u> - Strive for quality over quantity in both your clowning endeavors and personal commitments. Focusing on meaningful and impactful performances, as well as cherishing quality time with loved ones, contributes to a more enriching and fulfilling life.

As you navigate the continuous journey of growth as a clown, remember that the art of laughter is not just about the performances on stage but also about the continuous development of the performer behind the scenes. Embrace education, community, and a balanced approach to ensure that your clowning journey remains vibrant, joyful, and ever-evolving.

Chapter 12: Learning from the Greats

Delving into the rich history of clowning unveils a tapestry woven with the vibrant threads of iconic performers who have left an indelible mark on the world of laughter. In this chapter, we'll journey through time and explore the lives and legacies of famous clowns whose artistry has not only entertained but has also become a source of inspiration for aspiring performers. By studying the techniques, styles, and stories of these legends, you'll find a wellspring of knowledge to enrich your own clowning journey.

1. Joseph Grimaldi (1778–1837):

Widely regarded as the "Father of Clowning," Joseph Grimaldi, an English performer, set the foundation for modern clowning. His innovative use of white face makeup, colorful costumes, and physical comedy laid the groundwork for generations of clowns to come.

Source for Learning: Read "Memoirs of Joseph Grimaldi" to gain insights into the life and contributions of this foundational figure in clown history.

2. Emmett Kelly (1898–1979):

Known for his iconic hobo clown character "Weary Willie," Emmett Kelly brought a nuanced, melancholic humor to the circus ring. His ability to convey emotions through minimalistic gestures and expressions made him a master of silent comedy.

Source for Learning: Study performances by Emmett Kelly through video footage and documentaries to understand the subtleties of his unique style.

3. Charlie Chaplin (1889–1977):

While primarily recognized as a silent film star, Charlie Chaplin's character "The Tramp" exhibits many qualities of a classic clown. His masterful blend of physical comedy, pathos, and social commentary revolutionized the art of entertainment.

Source for Learning: Explore Chaplin's silent films, especially "City Lights" and "Modern Times," to witness his unparalleled comedic genius.

4. Red Skelton (1913–1997):

A versatile entertainer, Red Skelton was known for his beloved clown character, "Freddy the Freeloader." His comedic timing, playful antics, and ability to connect with audiences on a personal level solidified his place as a beloved clown.

Source for Learning: Watch episodes of "The Red Skelton Show" to witness his brilliant comedic performances and understand his approach to clowning.

5. Shirley Temple (1928–2014):

While primarily celebrated as a child star, Shirley Temple showcased exceptional clowning skills in her films. Her infectious energy, expressive face, and natural talent for physical comedy endeared her to audiences worldwide.

Source for Learning: Explore Shirley Temple's films, such as "Curly Top" and "Heidi," to observe her charming and whimsical approach to clowning.

6. Bill Irwin (1950–Present):

A contemporary master of clowning, Bill Irwin has seamlessly blended traditional clowning techniques with modern theatrical performances. His physical prowess, silent storytelling, and command of the stage make him a beacon for aspiring clowns.

Source for Learning: Attend Bill Irwin's live performances, if possible, and analyze his techniques in works like "Fool Moon" to witness the evolution of clowning in a contemporary context.

7. Coco the Clown (1900–1974):

Nicolai Poliakoff, known as Coco the Clown, was a British circus clown whose white face and distinctive grin became iconic. His mastery of physical comedy, coupled with a warm stage presence, made him a revered figure in the circus world.

Source for Learning: Explore archival footage and recordings of Coco the Clown's performances to glean insights into classic circus clowning.

Learning from the Greats:

Watch Performances: Explore performances of these iconic clowns, both live and recorded, to observe their techniques, timing, and stage presence.

Read Biographies: Delve into biographies, autobiographies, and documentaries about these legendary figures to gain a deeper understanding of their lives, influences, and contributions to the world of clowning.

Attend Workshops and Classes: Seek out workshops or classes that focus on the techniques and styles employed by famous clowns. Learning from experienced instructors can provide valuable insights.

Experiment and Personalize: Take inspiration from the greats but don't hesitate to experiment and infuse your own personality into your clowning style. The most memorable clowns are those who bring a unique, authentic touch to their performances.

By immersing yourself in the legacy of these legendary clowns, you embark on a journey of discovery and inspiration. Their timeless contributions serve as guideposts, offering lessons that can enrich your own clowning repertoire. Whether you're drawn to the classic circus clown, the silent film antics of Chaplin, or the contemporary brilliance of Bill Irwin, each iconic clown leaves behind a trail of laughter that beckons aspiring performers to join the ranks of those who have mastered the art of bringing joy to the world.

Chapter 13: Further Resources

Your journey into the world of clowning has just begun, and there's a wealth of knowledge and inspiration waiting for you to explore. Here are some additional resources that can guide you on your path to becoming a skilled clown artist:

Books and Publications:

- "The Art of Clowning" by Eli Simon
- "Clown: Readings in Theatre Practice" by John Davison
- "The Silent Clowns" by Walter Kerr

Online Learning Platforms:

InvisibleRopes.com: Our website is dedicated to all types of stage performance. From articles and tutorials to video demonstrations and interactive exercises, you'll find a treasure trove of resources to enhance your understanding and skills.

The Clown School (theclownschool.com) offers online courses for both beginners and experienced clowns.

Workshops and Classes:

Look for local theaters, art schools, and community centers that offer workshops and classes. These hands-on experiences can provide valuable insights and practical training.

Online Communities and Forums:

Join online communities and forums where fellow mime enthusiasts share tips, experiences, and resources. Engaging with others who share your passion can be both informative and motivating.

World Clown Association (worldclown.com): An international organization offering resources, events, and a community for professional and amateur clowns.

Clowns International (clownsinternational.org): A UK-based organization dedicated to the promotion and preservation of clowning traditions.

Documentaries and Films:

Explore documentaries and films that showcase the lives and work of renowned clowns. These visual resources can provide insight into the history, techniques, and impact of mime.

"King of Comedy" (1952) – A documentary on the life and career of Charlie Chaplin.

"Being There" (1979) – A film featuring the legendary clown Bill Irwin.

Whether you're flipping through the pages of a classic book, honing your skills with an online workshop, or connecting with like-minded individuals in a clowning forum, these resources are designed to be your allies in the pursuit of a more enriched and informed clowning experience. So, dive into the laughter-filled sea of resources, explore, learn, and let your journey in the art of clowning continue to unfold with boundless joy and discovery.

Conclusion

Wrapping up our exploration of clowning, it's time to take a breather and reflect on the journey. Whether you've been honking noses for years or are just stepping into oversized shoes, each laugh and pratfall has shaped your unique narrative. For those aspiring to don the wig and makeup, know that clowning isn't just about gags; it's about finding your stride in a quirky, joy-filled world. Embrace the oddities, pick up new tricks, and remember that every stumble is part of the dance. So, as you navigate the circus of life, may your nose stay red, your humor stay infectious, and may the echoes of your laughter linger long after the spotlight dims. Keep clowning, keep growing, and let the world be your big, whimsical canvas.

Printed in Great Britain
by Amazon